HUNTER AND NOAH VS. SASQUATCH

SASQUATCH CHRONICLES

BOOK 4

PATRICK TALMADGE

HANGAR 1 PUBLISHING

1

TINA'S FIRST THREE WEEKS WITH HUMANS

Those first few days of living with humans again were the toughest for Tina. She had very few memories of her first five years, which she'd spent among her own kind, back before the Sasquatch found her. The subsequent 170 years of living with the Sasquatch passed so fast it'd felt like only a few years. A few adjustments were needed in order to live with humans again. The Sasquatch had either been lucky or spent lots of time and energy finding Hunter's family, Tina thought. Having an annoying little brother was fun, and he acted like a little Sasquatch friend, which she thought was nice. Having a mom and dad made her feel safe and loved. Then there was Grandpa, who was just like the Sasquatch because he was always exploring, experimenting, learning, and joking. Oh... and that Hunter was something else.

There was something different about how he looked at her and how funny it made her feel. She really liked Hunter, but when they were near each other she felt funny. Sometimes all she wanted to do was be around Hunter and talk, because he was so interesting. She had overheard Mom say something about Hunter and her having a "crush" on each other. Tina didn't know what a crush was. and needed to do some research. Hunter was supposed to be her go-to person for questions about fitting in socially, but her instincts told her he was the last person to ask about this particular topic. This had to be one of those 'mother and daughter' talks, like Mom had mentioned a couple days ago. It was time for a sit down.

Mom listened to Tina tell her all about how Hunter made her feel, that she wanted to spend all her spare time with him, and that it was for some reason very important that Hunter liked her back. She went on to say how it made her feel unhappy if she saw Hunter talking to another girl. Basically, she was confused, and couldn't understand why she was being so weird and felt so funny. Having spent her whole life with Sasquatch, Tina had never experienced an attraction to another human. Mom knew Tina was having her first full-blown crush. Having birthed only sons, Mom never expected that she would ever have this conversation about crushes and first loves. Since her kids were both boys, Mom figured it would be their father who'd have 'the talk' with them, but now she had a daughter, and it was time.

"Oh my, Tina," said Mom. "I know what you're talking about, and what it feels like, although it has been a while since I had my first crush," Mom added, then reached out, took Tina's hand in hers, and held it tightly. "Tina, you have been alive much longer than I, but without human contact, and with how you have remained so young, you've never experienced the emotions that come with being around other humans. The funny feelings you have around Hunter are normal feelings that a 13-year-old girl has when she likes a 13-year-old boy. You will feel happy when he is around, and sad when he is gone. Sometimes he will make you mad, though he hasn't done a thing, and you can't figure out why you're mad at him. Humans call this a crush. And, for your information, Hunter is having the same feelings. The best thing you two can do is relax, enjoy each other's company, not take anything seriously, and play, play, play like the kids you are. But... well, I know you're almost 200 years old, Tina, but you are still a kid in your body, mind, and emotions, so go slowly and enjoy.

Mom took Tina clothes shopping at the mall after their talk. It would give them more time to talk relationship stuff and give Tina more experience in being around lots of humans. Tina loved the mall. The clothes, makeup, and food court dazzled her. The young boys and girls walking around the mall held most of her attention, though. Mom decided it would be a good idea to stop at the food court, so they could people watch. Mom chose peach ice cream for their treat, because she knew Tina liked peaches especially well. It was definitely a hit with Tina. The people watching proved to be the best teacher for Tina when it came to comprehending normal human social behavior. She watched people walk around the mall, stop at the food court, and eat. She saw every example of human social behavior, both good and bad, that day. Mom noticed the rude behavior or people that were mad, yelling, or fighting bothered her the most. Tina remained silent for the 2 hours they sat and watched, her peach ice cream melting while she observed from her chair. Mom knew there were going to be many questions after they left the mall, and Tina felt safe enough to ask her even the more difficult ones.

It was when the young boys Tina's age and couples were near that she was focused the most. Mom could almost hear the gears turning in her head and then catching and stopping when she had a question. Mom knew Tina would want to know why the couples' held hands and touched so much. OH, Mom was not looking forward to Tina's question of, "What the heck were they doing when they touched faces?" Mom really wasn't sure how she was going to explain kissing to a girl who was raised by the Sasquatch, since they are not very physical, and so she'd never even seen kissing. Even for a normal 13-year-old girl, kissing is often a huge source of anxiety, and those questions were the ones Mom knew were coming and also the ones she was dreading answering the most.

That's why Mom was so surprised when Tina didn't have many questions while they were driving home. Tina instead talked mostly about the rude people and explained she had not seen anger while living with the Sasquatch. It was difficult to see people yell at one another for her. As far as the couples holding hands and touching faces, Tina decided it was too early for her to learn about such things, and wanted to concentrate on learning at school, and running cross-country. When they got home, Mom was sure she let out the longest breath of relief ever once Tina left the room. Maybe having a daughter wasn't going to be so easy, thought Mom.

Tina settled in after that day, slowly got used to being

around Hunter, and accepted him as a brother. Now she knew it was a natural thing that humans went through, it wasn't too bad, but hormones would always have a bad reputation, as far as she was concerned. After the mall trip, Tina spent a couple hours a day studying human social interactions by watching social media videos and posts, then comparing them to how the people around her acted. Cross-country practice and walking around Tenino shopping were other ways she learned about normal human behavior.

2

SCHOOL FOR TINA

Mom and Dad felt it would be both easier and more fun if Tina went to Tenino Middle School with Hunter, even though she was educated well beyond middle school level. She could learn how to socialize with other kids there, under the guidance of Hunter. She would need to be coached about social norms before she could be around kids alone, though. Hunter, Noah, and Mom would need to help build a new personal history for Tina. Saying you came from the 1800s, and had lived with Sasquatch for 170 years would not exactly be the best way to begin the school year! Hunter's job was teaching her to avoid being bullied. Luckily, Tenino Middle School was a small-town school, and most of the kids were nice. But still, all it would take was one crazy comment about living with Sasquatch to turn nice kids into bullies, so maximum care and attention was paid to make sure her stories were straight.

The Sasquatch had provided the documents, but that was

only part of what was necessary. The rest entailed Tina, Hunter, and Noah keeping to the same story at school when talking to friends. The fabricated background story was that Tina's parents were lifelong best friends and had gone to high school with Hunter and Noah's mom and dad. When both families had their first born, they drew up papers to become godparents to each other's children. The story was that Tina's parents were killed in a car accident, while she was at school. Once Mom was sure the three kids had the story straight, she allowed them to venture away from the house without an adult.

Four weeks before school started, Mom got permission to give a tour of Tenino Middle School, meet teachers, and meet some of the other students that happened to be at school. Since they lived only three blocks away, the kids visited every day to build familiarity. Tina was enjoying herself, and feeling like being around so many kids would be exciting, when the cross-country coach walked up to Hunter to ask if he was signed up for the season, and if he had been training. Hunter assured Coach Ruud that he had been working out hard in the mountains by walking, running, swimming, and even doing lots of tree climbing for strength training.

"That does sound like you have really been preparing for the season Hunter," said Coach Ruud. "You're the team's leading runner, and I expect the team to vote for you to be team captain this year. Remember, being team captain is a big responsibility, and I know you can handle it, Hunter. Anyway, please excuse my manners," coach Rudd turned to Tina, "I am Coach Ruud, I coach cross country, and who are you?"

"Hello, Coach Ruud," Tina said, as she shook his extended

hand. "I have recently moved from Ohio to Tenino and will be spending my school year here. Hunter's parents were my parents' best friends when they were growing up, and they are my godparents. I lost my parents to an accident a few months ago... and their wishes were that, if anything ever happened to them, I should go live with Hunter and his family.

"I am very sorry for your loss, Tina, but I am sure that Hunter and his family will help you through this difficult time. Ohio is a long way from little Tenino, but we are a friendly little town. By the way, you seem quite fit, Tina, and you are hanging around with my best runner! Is there any chance you plan on running cross country for our girls' team?" I, uhhh... sorry, Tina, you will have to excuse me for being so forward about asking. We are a small town, with very few girls to fill the team's roster, so as a coach I need to constantly look for talent," he said, with earnest eyes.

"Honestly, I am flattered you asked! I had not considered running cross country, because I do not know much of the sport, but I have spent many years running on the mountain trails back home."

"Oh my, that sounds like you certainly have a love for the sport, Tina. You can talk to Hunter about it, and maybe he will take you for a run on our team's cross-country course. It is almost all in the woods, lots of hills, no cars, and smells like heaven," said Coach Rudd, with a pride in his voice.

"I look forward to running on the course with Hunter," said Tina. "Running on the team sounds fun, too. It'll be a fun way to meet new people since I am new here, so I am sure you can count on me joining the team."

Coach Ruud shook Tina's hand and said, "Let me be the first to welcome you to the team," then walked off with a big smile.

Hunter was silent the whole time coach Ruud talked to Tina. He could hardly believe she was going to be on the cross-country team. The two of them would be spending lots of time at practice, at meets, and traveling to and from races. This was going to be the best season ever, he thought, then he wondered how fast she ran. The coach was right about taking her on a run. He decided that right now was the best time to find out if Tina was in good shape, and see how fast she was, so he asked, "Tina, do you want to go home, change into running gear, and run the cross-country course?"

"That would be so fun, Hunter. I haven't run in the woods in weeks, and it would be nice to see the course with you," she said, unable to hide the blush on her cheeks.

Luckily, Hunter didn't notice Tina blushing. He was too busy thinking about how hard the cross-country course was, even for him, and was worried it would be too much for Tina. He planned on going slow and taking it easy, to ensure she could handle it. The kids got home, changed into running gear, and jogged across town to the starting line of the course.

Tenino is a small town, so it was only a half mile to the starting line. Hunter was impressed by how fast Tina was jogging already. He was sure she was as fast as any runner they had on the girls' team, which was going to make Coach Ruud very happy. Once they got to the starting line, Hunter showed Tina how to do the warmup stretches and sprints. The course was very well marked, and Hunter had Tina lead the way and set the pace so that he wouldn't run too fast for her.

Tina was not just fast, she was very fast. Hunter was the fastest kid on his middle school team—and in the district—and she wore him out on his home course! Hunter was sure he could beat Tina, but she would beat every girl on his team... and maybe in the state. She would likely beat most of the boys, too. Tina was a budding cross country star, and didn't even know it. The boys' and girls' teams were going to be champs this year for sure, thought Hunter.

The next day, Hunter took Tina to the cross-country practice. Much to the delight of Coach Ruud, she demonstrated that not only was she faster than all the girls, but she was faster than all the boys, except Hunter, and he wasn't too far ahead. The coach smiled, knowing Tina would push Hunter and the rest of the team to be faster. She was also a natural leader, and was great at encouraging the other teammates. Especially the boys she beat in practice. She told them she trained year-round back home and that, if they did also, they would easily get faster than her.

"Well, looks like the Tenino Tigers are going all the way this year, kids! So, it's time to pick them feet up and put them down faster if we want to win district!" Coach Ruud yelled. "Now I want all of you to run two easy laps on the team course. No racing, everyone stays together, and I want talking and support from, and for, everyone. Okay, out and back, go! And enjoy yourselves!"

Coach Ruud watched his runners jog away, and thought that this may be the year he'd retire. If the boys' and girls' teams both won, he would have reached the pinnacle of coaching and could retire as a true winner. Yes, this was going to be a good year.

After the workout, Hunter and Tina jogged home to get lunch. Mom was happy that Tina was going to be on the team, and surprised that she was so fast. Hunter told Mom that Coach Ruud got really funny when he realized how fast Tina was. It must have dawned on him that they could win the state championships, for both girls and boys, and he kind of freaked out.

"I was thinking... if we do win both state championships, would coach Ruud move to be the high school coach?" Hunter asked. "Even though we will only be here for another two years, it would be great to have Coach Ruud coach this year, and our first year in high school cross-country, before we leave."

"I don't really know if the coach will go or not, but I do know you and Tina need to get back to school and get signed up for your classes, or you will be getting last pickings! Furthermore, I don't care what the Sasquatch learning center can teach, you three will be going to public school here until we move to the Sasquatch valley in two years."

"Alright, Mom, we hear and obey your orders. As soon as we shower up and grab a bite to eat, we will head over and get signed up for classes. I, for one, plan on taking underwater basket weaving for sure!" Hunter said, with a chuckle, as he skipped out of the kitchen to clean up.

"It may take longer than the 170 years I spent with the Sasquatch to understand boys," Tina said, with a sigh and a shake of her head as she left to clean up. "Sometimes I think the boredom of 170 years with the Sasquatch wasn't so bad, after how dull spending the afternoon with boys can be," she added, under her breath.

After living with her two boys, their dad, and their grandpa, Mom was in full agreement with Tina. Although, if she'd lived with the Sasquatch for 170 years like Tina had, she would have spent lots of time in the Sasquatch learning center. A few PhDs in psychology and in animal behavior should help her understand those 'boys,' she thought, with a laugh.

Tina was surprised by the broad variety of class choices Hunter's school offered. Since she was already at a college level understanding of math and science, Tina focused on classes that would help her live with humans. She thought taking a foreign language would help her understand and communicate with those from other cultures, so she took Spanish. The Sasquatch don't have music like the humans, only small soft playing drums. Oh, and they hum, but do not sing. Tina liked the sounds the flute made the most, so she signed up for band with the goal of learning to play the flute. Humans relied on computers more than Sasquatch, so Tina took a computer class. Tenino Middle School also offered FFA (Future Farmers of America), and Tina thought that would be a great way to do some of the gardening she so loved, and to be around some of the animals the kids would raise.

It was her final class choice that made the most sense for Tina's life with humans - Psychology 101, and she planned on taking it every quarter until they moved back to the Sasquatch valley. That meant she had two years of living in Tenino, going to school, and learning everything possible about her kind before they moved, and she was going to make the most of every second. Tina had always felt happy with the Sasquatch... but also a bit out of place. Here, with Hunter and his family in Tenino, she felt at home. Even Noah was wonderful, even if he was a little stinker at times, and she was happy to call him her brother.

Much to Noah's displeasure, Mom made him take classes in the public school. She told him he needed a social life with kids his age, so he was going. Because he was so advanced, he was moved up one grade, into sixth grade. This also allowed him to be in middle school with Hunter and Tina. The middle school had a larger selection of classes, so he wouldn't be quite as bored. Mom and Noah agreed that he could go part time. He needed to take at least two classes a quarter. For the first quarter, he took advanced math, geography, and an art class. Noah saw the pottery class and said he had always wanted to try making ceramic pots since watching the Sasquatch make them.

3

NEW SASQUATCH TECH COMPANIES FORMED

Dad was going to be running the new electricity generating paint company, but that was just the beginning of the eco-tech centered companies that were going to be coming out. The company Mom liked most was the one that built vertical gardens in people's yards, on their rooftops and walls, and even on boats. Each garden was designed to produce year-round, with very little time needed to care for it, yet a typical garden was capable of feeding a family of 4. The most ambitious new company would be making homes grown from specially developed trees. Except they weren't exactly trees. The Sasquatch developed these super-fast-growing vines that grow into houses. Within a matter of 4 to 5 weeks, the vines grew into a tightly woven box that could be manipulated to form rooms, windows, walls, and even watertight ceilings. Once fully grown, their leaves act like solar panels capable of generating all the electricity the home needs. These homes were different from the tree homes. The tree homes they were going to live in were taller, and generally located near rivers, whereas the vine homes were shorter, and made to be in neighborhoods. Dad was glad they were going to be by the irrigation culvert and river, rather than in a neighborhood.

Once the property around the valley was bought, Dad's company, with the help of the Sasquatch, started building manufacturing centers and office buildings for the new companies. Every time Dad went to inspect the work on the new buildings, Hunter, Noah, and Tina went as well. Dad couldn't be sure, but he'd swear Noah would sneak off to the Sasquatch learning lab whenever he came along. The problem was that the ability to manipulate time made it hard to tell. Noah could be gone for two months in his time, and only 30 minutes in mine, thought Dad. Plus, Mom was right, don't over think and don't ask Noah questions you don't really want to know the answers to.

While Dad toured the building sites, Tina showed Hunter around the Sasquatch village and caves. It was that little smarty Noah that was always so secretive, and never really answered the question of where he was when they were up in the valley. Dad wasn't worried though, because the Sasquatch would never allow anything to happen to Noah. Well, they had allowed him to grow fur like theirs... although, in their defense, having fur like theirs isn't in any way harmful. Actually, he looked kind of cute, and I'll never forget the way Mom laughed after seeing Noah covered in fur, thought Dad, smiling to himself.

The building on Dad's tour one day was a manufacturing

plant that made machines that could extract water from the air, so a house or building would not need water pipes or have water bills. The Sasquatch wanted every human to have access to safe water, and developed these for people who do not have clean water, or clean water that was close by. To Dad's amazement, when he entered the building, he saw Noah talking to a half dozen men and Sasquatch.

"Oh, hi Dad," said Noah when he saw him. "I was just going over a few design changes for the electrical panel on the unit."

"Design changes? Electrical panels? You're pretty heavily involved... does this happen to have something to do with you disappearing every time we come up to the valley?"

"Yes, it does, Dad," answered Noah. "Once I learned that there were people, especially kids, that never had access to clean water or enough water, I made it my goal to learn everything I could to bring water to them. The Sasquatch gave me the education, and now we are building a plant to make machines that will bring water to everyone, and it will cost them nothing. Yes, nothing. This plant was designed to make these units at no cost to the consumer. The Sasquatch agreed with me that water should be a right, not a privilege, so it will be free," Noah said, with great pride.

"Noah, I am at a complete loss for words at your incredible gift to the world. You have selflessly thought about others and devoted yourself to the benefit of others with no reward for yourself," Dad told Noah, and gave him a big hug.

"Thank you, Dad. I hope you remember that pride when you see the other companies I had a hand in designing. Also, remember the Sasquatch bought into my ideas and are behind them, so they can't be too bad," Noah said, with a slight nervousness in his voice.

"Any chance you want to talk about those new companies, Noah?" asked Dad.

"You know, Dad, I think we should cross those bridges when we get to them. I still have a lot of planning changes to go over, and really should be getting back to work now, so I don't hold these nice beings up any longer," Noah said, then turned back to his group.

Dad knew better than to try to pry any more information out of Noah. He was correct, the Sasquatch wouldn't allow anything that was dangerous, or a waste of time or resources, so he decided to not think any more about it, and resigned himself to hopefully being happily surprised by Noah's new companies when they came to fruition. With Noah's imagination, he might try to invent hats with propellers! Come to think of it, that does sound fun, and I know it is nothing I should talk to Noah about, or he will try to make them, thought Dad. Maybe I'll bring it up later with him, when I get bored.

The Sasquatch walked everywhere, so they had no need for any sort of vehicle. Any time they needed to carry large loads or move things larger than they could carry, they used antigravity lifters. Some of these lifters were small, and used to move lighter loads like rocks and dirt, while other lifters were capable of lifting whole buildings. The Sasquatch realized humans needed to have vehicles to move faster and easier, and that the most popular modes of transportation for human kids were electric bikes, scooters, and go-carts. The adults also liked the kids' electric vehicles, but needed bigger electric cars and trucks. The Sasquatch-enhanced electric vehicle companies were going to be a success.

It was going to take many visits for Dad to do a complete inspection of all the electric vehicle manufacturing plants, but they were always the most interesting. Dad could only imagine how people were going to react to the new electric vehicles they were going to be making. Imagine their surprise when they learned that none of these new vehicles ever needed to be plugged in or have fuel added! To top that news off, there would be no purchase price on any of the vehicles. In fact money was not a part of Sasquatch culture, in any form. Everything in the Sasquatch world is free, and they like to create environments that are self-supporting.

4

TREE HOMES BEGINNING TO SHAPE UP

When the Sasquatch initially suggested using Hunter and Noah's tree home Idea, Grandpa and Dad fell about laughing. But once the Sasquatch showed them the modifications, both agreed that even Mom—who by her own admittance was a comfort queen—would give her house away in a second to move into one of the newly designed, highly modified tree homes that were decked out with incredible Sasquatch technology. There going to be so many comforts built in that no one would be able to resist living in them.

It would take almost two years to grow each home, due to the complexity of the growing process. The Sasquatch genetically modified and programmed the growth of the trees so that they included different rooms, hallways, open walkways, bathrooms, and even living rooms with large windows that opened. As the trees grow, bubbles would form in the main trunk and larger branches. The bubbles then would continue to grow in size, until big enough to be the rooms they were designed to be. Once grown to size, all the trimmings and final pieces, like shelves, doors, and windows, bathroom fixtures, and kitchen appliances would be grown.

Sasquatch technology is so highly advanced that not only can they grow trees into houses and all their composite parts, but the genetically engineered plant-based machines can make water and electricity, too. The biggest surprise was that they were able to genetically engineer devices like the food synthesizers and 3D printers, and do so using only genetically engineered plants. The plant-based machines almost always generated all the electricity they needed to operate. Sometimes the machines needed to draw extra power from the house or building where they were located and, in some instances, an extra solar power unit would need to be added to account for heavy usage.

Dad knew there was no doubt that Mom was going to love the new Sasquatch tree homes, because not only did they have every comfort of a normal human home—such as a bathroom, kitchen, heat, air-conditioning—but they came with a few over the top surprises, too. Mom loved open floor plans, high ceilings, lots of windows, and big master bathrooms, and Dad was certain everything she wanted, needed, and wished for was included in the tree home designs, as well as much more.

The biggest surprise that most kids and adults would go crazy over was that each person in the house would have their own personal robot. The new robots were designed to be the perfect helpers. They could do any chore a human could, such as dishes, taking out the garbage, sweeping or mopping, but also ordering food from the grocery store, and cooking virtual meals. Each person's robot would accompany them whenever and wherever the person chooses to go. These personal robots would be great for kids due to being such wonderful teachers and safe babysitters. The houses would also have a few of what the Sasquatch called, 'domestic robots' that would be used mostly for cleaning. Each domestic robot was designed for a specialized purpose. Some kept the floors clean or washed windows, and other robots would work outside around the tree, maintaining the food gardens which could free up humans to do whatever else they may choose.

An important detail that would make living in a tree home a truly comfortable experience was the elevators. These were especially important in Hunter and Noah's house, because it was 200 feet off the ground, and would be too much work to climb. There would be as many elevators in each home as the residents wanted. Each elevator was to be built from a plant that raises and lowers depending on where you stand on the special leaf that was built like a box without a top. Relatives of the Venus Fly Trap, the Sasquatch genetically modified the plants to be bigger.... and no, they do not eat people, they can only move up and down. Dad was fairly certain that Mom was going to be happiest about the robots and elevators. Moving her out of Tenino wasn't going to be a big problem, for sure, thought Dad. He could see Mom riding the elevator down to the kitchen, asking the robot to make her some coffee and a fruit cup, and then relaxing on one of the tree's balconies 40 or 140 feet off the ground. Mom was going to be in heaven.

The Sasquatch are more social than humans, and took that into consideration when spacing the tree homes. Regardless of whether each was a taller tree home or a shorter one, the spacing between them was just far enough to ensure privacy as well as an unobstructed view from a deck on each house to a deck on other houses, so the families could talk whenever they wanted. All houses also had audio-visual and communication stations on each deck. This would allow for movie watching, schoolwork, computer surfing, or just talking to neighbors from your deck, while relaxing and barbecuing. The idea of a barbecue was foreign to the Sasquatch, because they don't eat meat, but when they were shown how to barbecue vegetables, a few of them were brave enough to try them, and many actually loved them enough to come to barbecue parties!

5

FIRST PEOPLE MOVE INTO TREE HOMES

The tree which Hunter and Noah modified, then lived in for 17 days, was now nothing like it was back then after the Sasquatch were done with their extensive changes. Hunter added running water and was able to supply warm water for Mom, and a few covered nests, but the Sasquatch made the tree so fantastic and loaded with fantastic features! It all would make sure Mom was so happy she'd never want to leave. There was plenty of hot water, many elevators, and sitting gardens that also grew food off of every room. The Sasquatch had grown the tree in the two years they had been working on it. The top deck level used to be 40 feet above the valley floor, but now the tree was 200 feet tall and had so many rooms and decks it would take Mom days to visit them all. Noah was sure that Mom was going to get lost, so he made sure there was an emergency robot following her around to every room, until she could find her way.

The tree homes that were made for other people in the same style as Hunter and Noah's were honestly not quite as fancy, but were still loaded with features that no regular home had. Every home, regardless of the size, was completely off-grid and self-sustaining. Every home made its own water, grew its own food, generated its own power, and took care of all waste which was recycled, because the homes were closed systems. A closed system means that nothing needs to be brought into it, like food or power, and that each house takes care of all its own waste. With the 3D printers, all clothing could also be made at home.

Mom had some idea the tree home was going to be high tech, but didn't realize how much tech there was going to be, or how high it was. The ground floor entrance was a simple set of three steps up to a covered porch that led to the front door, and that slid into the side of the wall when Dad asked the control panel next to the door to "Open the front door, please." Mom was impressed with the automatic door, but not as impressed as when she saw the main living room as she walked in the front door. Mom had not really paid much attention to the size of the tree as they'd approached their tree home. Well, she was now standing in a room that was at least 30 feet in diameter! This was the largest living room she had ever been in, and this one was inside a tree.

Noah had the honor of giving Mom a tour of their new home, and did so with great pride with the knowledge that he'd had a great deal to do with the planning of that home, along with Hunter, Grandpa, Dad, and the Sasquatch. After Mom had gotten used to the room size, Noah began showing her the 10 elevators on that floor. Each elevator went to a different part of the tree above. Most elevators were only good for two to three floors, though, and their new home had 10 floors, covering 200 feet. There were two floor levels that had open ceilings that were 20 to 40 feet. These were used as open spaces, and could be used for all sorts of playing when there were three kids in the house.

The next level Noah showed Mom was the kitchen. That was where Mom met the first robots... and where she really got excited! They cooked, cleaned, and performed basic tasks like fetching a phone, book, or food. When Mom found out that the robots could not only play music like a radio but also sing and play their own music, she vowed to sleep there. The balcony off of the kitchen was the biggest in the tree home. It could hold a table big enough for 12 people. Mom was beyond excited, because not only did she now have the room to entertain, but she had unlimited kitchen help. Dad joked that Mom may never spend time in any other portion of the tree home!

Hunter and Noah shared a level. There was a center room that had a table and an entertainment and study area. Noah and Hunter each had their own side, and each side was three times the size of a normal bedroom, with a 15-foot ceiling. Both bedrooms had a balcony that let in fresh air and allowed them, especially Noah, to use a safety line to jump out. Recognizing this, Mom made it mandatory that Noah was not allowed to have a bedroom that was too far off the ground, since he would be jumping out as often as possible. Noah tried to argue for a higher level, but Mom won, and they ended up with a room only 40 feet off the ground. Noah stated that he "Could jump from higher anytime he wanted anyway" and that comment earned Noah a serious Mom stare.

Tina got a whole floor to herself, two levels above the boys. She had a beautiful apartment. Her entertainment system was on the wall by her balcony, and she had a full kitchen area with an electric fireplace. She had fallen in love with the ones they had in the Tenino home. Tina was slightly cold much of the time she lived with the Sasquatch, because she lacked fur. Now, on those cool mornings or cold winter days, she could snuggle up in front of her fireplace and keep toasty warm.

The last floor inside the tree home was Mom and Dad's room. It was a masterful marriage of technology with beauty and comfort. Every square inch of the interior was a soft moss. Noah explained that the moss was their source of light and heat, and that she could change its color to any color or pattern she chose. The bed looked like a royal four-poster bed and a giant moss pillow.

Mom was standing there in awe, staring at their bedroom, when Noah suggested she and Dad try laying on the bed for size. The pair lay down, and immediately you could see huge smiles spreading across their faces.

"Oh my gosh," said Dad. "As soon as I lay down, I became almost weightless."

"This is the most amazing bed," exclaimed Mom. "Normally, my back feels a bit tight and painful when I lay in bed, but this bed makes me feel lighter than a feather, and there is no pain or pressure on my back."

"Well, Mom, if you think the bed is nice then just wait until you see your personal bathroom," said Noah. "Now, if I may introduce you to your new friend and personal helper, Robot 753," Noah added with a smile, as he led a robot by the hand towards Mom.

The robot almost had a human face and stood 5-foot-tall. It was cute, looked like it was perpetually smiling, and there was a sort of fuzzy synthetic hair on its head.

"What? Do you mean this robot is my new friend and personal helper?" asked Mom.

"I am what Noah said I was, Mom. I am your personal assistant, and hopefully your new friend, because it would be more rewarding being with you, and being your friend, than simply your assistant," said the robot. "That is, if I may call you Mom. One more thing, Mom, you can name me anything you choose. I was given the name 753 because I was the 753rd robot off the line, and I would very much appreciate you picking a new name for me that you love," The robot finished, then stood silently.

"This is the most exciting day in my life! Okay, maybe minus getting married and giving birth twice," Mom said, with wide eyes as she stared at 753.

"Does that mean I make you happy?" asked 753.

"Yes, you have made me very happy! And I can tell we will become best friends, also. Now, we need to come up with a name for you... wait, do you have a name you would like to be called?"

"I did not know I would be asked my opinion... Tanya. I'd like to be called Tanya. I love that name, and would have picked it over 753 if I could have."

"I have been surprised many times today, but this is the

biggest and the best," said Mom. "For now on, you are not 753, but Tanya, and I am certain you are my new best friend."

Tanya stepped up to Mom and hugged her. Mom noticed Tanya somehow felt like a human, and was even warm to the touch.

Noah, as usual, broke the mood by saying, "Alright, time to cut the mushy stuff and get to the top."

Everyone started at Noah to point out his rudeness. As usual, he didn't pay attention, and headed to one of the elevators to go up.

Tanya laughed, grabbed Mom's hand, and said, "Come with me and I will show you the view," then led Mom to an elevator.

The view from the top was break taking. Their tree was the tallest in the valley by 50-feet, and their view was unmatched. You could see for miles, and on a clear day Mt. Rainier was visible. Dad suggested that breakfast up there would have to become a normal occasion. Mom was a bit nervous about falling without her specially made Carhartt's on, but Tanya informed her that the treetop had a built-in safety force field that would prevent anyone or anything from falling over the edge.

"There is no way I could have imagined a home as beautiful and fantastic as this," said Mom. "I want to thank every one of you for all your work towards making this dream come true, and that includes you, Tanya."

After much hugging and sightseeing from the tree top, the group went down to check out Grandpa's tree home. It was going to be a total surprise to everyone but Grandpa, because he was the one who'd designed it. Most everyone prioritized comfort and high-tech... but Grandpa went with 'pure fit and function,' as he put it, or 'nothing but a workshop with a bed and a bathroom' as Mom called it. Grandpa's tree home was at ground level, was only one level, and basically looked like a giant barrel with a tree growing out of the top. Grandpa said he didn't need any silly comforts taking up valuable workspace, because there was a limit to what the Sasquatch could grow inside a single level tree home. He needed a bed, bathroom, and a climate-controlled shop he could work in at any time of the day, night, or year, regardless of the weather.

Like most people, Grandpa had a TV style monitor. The difference was that Grandpa's monitor took up a whole wall. It measured 10 feet tall, and 20 feet wide. Grandpa insisted he needed it so he could "do design work from the comfort of my favorite chair."

It's not fair how Grandpa got one and I didn't," Noah said. "I need one like it for my video games."

"We could do homework on it, also," Hunter added.

Mom reminded them that they didn't actually ever have homework, then said, "Nice try boys."

"What if we have the Sasquatch grow one on the cliff wall by our pond in the grotto, so all of us kids can watch movies or play group games?" asked Tina. "That is where most of us kids play, so having a giant monitor there would be fun."

Noah and Hunter were in full agreement with Tina's suggestion, and Mom thought that was a fantastic idea, and that it would keep her tree home a bit quieter.

"Next time I am at the Sasquatch main lab, I will give them the suggestion," said Grandpa.

Mom decided it was time for the family to go tree home to tree home and greet the neighbors, so suggested everyone collect flowers to give as tree warming gifts. The whining could be heard for miles, but one look from Mom closed mouths and got feet moving.

6

HUNTER AND NOAH TEACH OTHER KIDS

Hunter, Noah, and Tina took special classes from the Sasquatch that would help them be better teachers. This was because the Sasquatch wanted the three of them to teach the new kids that were going to be moving into the Sasquatch valley area to live in harmony with the forest. They wanted the children to learn to live off the land, in the way Hunter and Noah had for 17 days. To make it more fun and safe, the Sasquatch and Grandpa reengineered the Carhartt coveralls to have more cool features and gadgets. These included making the coveralls automatically seal watertight in an emergency, as well as making them insulated for freezing temperatures, and buoyant. The safety lines were also modified to automatically deploy and attach to something, in the event of a fall, be over 100 feet long, and were optimized to be much faster at climbing up. The coveralls exterior material was swapped out for a bullet proof fabric, and in an emergency like a bear attack, the modified Carhartt's would also automatically inflate to a size too large for the bear to bite. This not only prevented the bear from being able to bite the wearer, but also made the wearer too big to drag away. To power all those new electronics, the bullet proof exterior material was created so that it generated electricity like a solar panel and stored extra power for when there was no light. In the event of a really big emergency, the suits were equipped with batteries in each boot heel that could power the Carhartt's for up to a week in the absence of any light.

Once the new kids arrived and moved in, they spent the first few weeks training with Hunter, Noah, and Tina, while their parents were getting settled in at work and home. The first day was training in the new Carhartt coveralls, so that every kid could be safer while learning survival skills. The suits would protect them from the cold river when they were gathering clams and crawdads. The built-in collection bags were used for gathering mushrooms, nuts, and berries. The Carhartt's bulletproof construction certainly would come in handy while gathering the food, because it could easily protect them from thorns and sharp rocks and sticks. The automatic inflation features, along with being bulletproof, were also especially helpful when gathering berries in the fall, when the bears were the most dangerous.

Hunter, Noah, and Tina each focused on teaching different aspects of survival, although they all helped each other with the various lessons. Noah, of course, focused heavily on the safety line system. With complete modesty, Noah said his class was voted the most favorite class in the whole three weeks. Except for a few individuals afraid of heights, Noah was correct, since most kids and adults enjoyed jumping from trees and slowly floating to the ground with the inertial reel, then quickly climbing back up using the electric winch. Mom was one of those individuals that loved jumping with the safety system, so much so that she and Noah came to the practice course at least once a week to play.

Once the new kids had mastered the features of their suits, they spent the rest of the three weeks in the woods, learning to live off the land, from Hunter, Noah, and Tina. There was no danger involved, because each kid had their personal robot tagging along, and a few Sasquatch and humans as additional chaperones. Unless there was an emergency, the chaperones were not allowed to talk to or help the kids. The chaperones were there purely as a safety measure.

All of the new Carhartt coveralls had fishing gear built in. While the Sasquatch themselves do not eat fish, they understand that humans do since they need the protein, so they included that fishing gear. The coveralls also had both a slingshot and a bow with arrows built in. The Sasquatch did not feel they were needed for hunting or protection, but they felt that learning how to use both a slingshot and a bow would help the children's confidence and build survival skills. Each child was also required to do a moderate amount of exercise to encourage better overall health.

Over the three weeks the kids were training with Hunter, Noah, and Tina, they would be living off the land, by their own efforts. Everything the kids need they would have to provide for themselves. They would gather their own food, water, and make their own shelter with a sleeping nest. They would learn to build a few different shelter designs, the particulars of which being dependent on the time of year and the location. Summer shelters were the simplest, usually featuring open tops, whereas the winter shelters had to be waterproof and insulated. Some of the kids decided to build more complex designs, and spent the extra time needed to build a woven basket style shelter. They would find a grove of young willow trees, which they could easily bend the soft flexible branches of to weave a basket. Once the basket was complete, they'd interweave smaller branches, moss, and ferns to make it wind and rain proof. After they finished the basket part, moss, grass, and ferns were added to the bottom to make it as soft as a bird's nest. Usually, they then added a side opening to climb in and out, which kept the rain out as well. Noah chose to design and build a basket style shelter with the entrance in the bottom of the nest. He put the entrance in the center of the basket bottom, so he could hook his safety line to a branch at the top of the basket and jump. When he wanted to go back up, he used the electric motor. Noah may have spent years studying with the Sasquatch, but he was still a 10-year-old kid at heart!

The Sasquatch were impressed Hunter had made solar ovens using protein bar wrappers and an emergency space blanket. They determined that having the material to build an emergency solar oven should be included in the essentials that were part of the modified Carhartt coveralls. The Sasquatch used materials that were as light as tinfoil but as strong as steel. The material was rolled up into a thin tube, which slipped into a small pouch in the seam of the upper thigh of the coveralls.

The material was attached to two chopstick-like things that were bound together and opened like scissors to hold the material like a hammock. The Sasquatch rarely heated food, but knew humans needed to cook food and boil water, so they built the best gear for the kids to meet that need. The adults also had the modified coveralls, but their training was limited, because most would not be playing in the forest like the kids.

7

THE PERILS OF FOOD GATHERING

Tina was the lead instructor for the mushroom, berry, and nut gathering training. First and foremost, the training focused on being observant. Mainly, they were taught to look for all sources of danger and at all times. Always pay attention to where you're walking and keep your eyes, ears, and noses open to any dangerous animals, especially bears, was the fundamental lesson. They were pretty much the only dangerous animal. Most other animals would run away. Only once did a kid make the mistake of petting one of the black cats with the white stripe, which smelled very bad. Well, that kid thought a skunk was a cat, tried to pet it, and he got sprayed. From that stinky point on, the Sasquatch included a skunk detection system in the emergency protection software of the suit so that, if the suit detected a skunk, it would warn the wearer so they could avoid it.

Hunter's training specialty was when the real fun and

laughter began. Hunter was the lead instructor in river food gathering, which meant fish, crawfish, and freshwater clams. First of all, the coveralls floated, were waterproof, insulated, and could self-inflate in the event of an accident. In a worst-case scenario, the suits would shoot a safety line to a tree or rock to stop the wearer from being washed downstream. That meant it was fun and carefree to play with in the water. They could also be an accident waiting to happen, though, because the Carhartt's were a bit heavy. This made them clumsy to walk in, especially in the water. And this could cause someone to be more likely to fall. Falling in the coveralls isn't an issue at all. The padding and instant automatic inflation means you will not get hurt if you fall, even on land. Of course, you can't get hurt falling in the water either, but the coverall's buoyancy can lead to other problems. Fast moving water tends to wash people downstream unless they're firmly anchored. Deep water was another problem, because the suits just want to float, so going underwater to get a freshwater clam could be difficult, and very funny if the wearer got washed downstream!So, as wonderful as the Sasquatch coveralls were, that buoyancy could get annoying. It also became the source of most of the laughter during training. Even Hunter, Noah, and Tina—despite their considerable experience with the coveralls—had their own funny moments getting wet. The chaperones made sure they were close when the new kids went into the water for the first time in their coveralls. It's during times like this when humans realize how gentle and fun loving the Sasquatch truly are. They enjoyed sitting by the river while the kid's practiced. Sasquatch love laughing, and sometimes they can be loud, which should be expected from 8-foot-tall 700 pound beings… but can be a surprise to a first-time listener. Especially if there is a large group.

Hunter's instruction consisted of gathering freshwater clams and crawdads in the water, and lasted at least 3 days and was continued on a daily basis for normal food gathering. But it was the first day's practice in the river that made everyone laugh the hardest. It would be an understatement to say both Sasquatch and humans enjoyed bringing lunch to the river and laughing as the kids tried walking in the river. Many children had their feet washed out from under them and were sent head over heels downstream until they were able to stop themselves, or their coveralls did it automatically. There was no chance of getting hurt, but the chance of a sore stomach from laughing was a looming possibility!

The fishing part of Hunter's instruction wasn't quite as entertaining as clam hunting, but was a necessary skill for the kids to learn how to live off of the land. Most of the kids picked it up quickly. The Sasquatch engineered fishing gear was fantastic. It was feather light, and the reels were electric and used a catapult like system to cast with pinpoint accuracy. Hunter showed the kids one of the computerized fishing lures, which featured a camera and a motor they could control with their phone, smart watch, or smart glasses. The Sasquatch loved to include as many gadgets in their tech as possible, and although they did not fish, they thought it might be fun to be able to control where the fishing lure went, and then see underwater as it was controlled.

At the end of the weeks of training, the kids' parents joined them in the forest for a weekend of living off the land. Everyone was in their Carhartt's and fully prepared to live as a forest animal, forging for the food they needed, and making beds out of forest materials. It was a wonderful way for the kids to show-case their newfound skills and have a wonderful bonding time with their families. The Sasquatch always joined in on the fun and made sure to bring a few surprises. One weekend, the Sasquatch brought fireflies they had genetically modified to be the size of chickens! They cast so much light at night, that the Sasquatch were forced to take them back to the village so that people could get some sleep!

The adult Sasquatch and humans watched the kids play for hours in perfect harmony. It was easy to see that Sasquatch and humans were going to be able to coexist easily and thrive. The elder Sasquatch talked of times gone by when the humans and Sasquatch used to sit under the stars together just like that.

8

SASQUATCH FACTORIES BEGIN MANUFACTURING

Most every operation in the new factories was automated, meaning that very few personnel were required for manufacturing. Most employees worked in offices, or on the road in sales. Robots brought the raw materials to one side of the factory, then they did the manufacturing in the middle of the factory, and finally the robots shipped it out to the other side of the factory. Even the trucks were driverless autonomous vehicles. Humans were spared the dangerous, boring jobs whenever possible. With their incredibly long lives, the Sasquatch made sure work was enjoyable and rewarding. They valued family time, and having a social life, so their workdays were short and only 3 days out of the week were spent working, at most.

One of the most unusual products a Sasquatch factory makes is dog houses. These were not your ordinary, run of the mill, wooden dog houses. No... these dog houses were solar powered, with lights, water, heat, air-conditioning, and memory foam beds! Every doghouse had a door with a special electronic lock that only the dog who lived in that particular house could open. All dogs had a special, corresponding collar with an electronic tag that operated the lock. Locking dog houses were popular because they protected the dogs, their toys, and especially their food. Having a non-locking doghouse with food inside would attract pests, and even bears. The food dispensers were automatic, and the food sealed away, but it was best to keep everything but the dogs out of their houses.

Most adults guessed correctly when they said some of the kids would want these doghouses for their personal forts, because they were so nice. All they had to do was change from dog food to human food, and the kids were set to play. It probably doesn't need to be said, but some of the kids didn't care if they changed the food, because the dog food was so delicious and healthy!

When people talk about the weirdest Sasquatch factories, they are usually referring to the factories that make robots. As with all of them, the robot factories were automated, and most of the work was done by robots. Every component of each robot could be made by robots, assembled by them completely, then shipped by them to their final destination. Virtually every level of Sasquatch robotics was autonomous, from the little floor cleaning ones to the personal assistance robots that teach. Every robot was capable of understanding and responding to human speech. Even the water faucets in kitchen and bathroom sinks responded to verbal commands. To get water, you just needed to say something like, "Hey, faucet, can you please give me one quart of 115-degree water," or, "hey, faucet, can you run warm hand washing water for 15 seconds please?"

What makes the robot manufacturing factory seem so weird to some people, is watching robots building robots. Although the robots designed by the Sasquatch were totally safe and docile, some people still worried that they could rise up against the humans. This kind of thinking always made the Sasquatch laugh and say something along the lines of how humans spend more time worrying about what could go wrong, than enjoying what they were doing. The Sasquatch language has no word for anxiety, since they never feel that way. Grandpa always said, "The Sasquatch are too smart and too big to worry about anything."

One thing the Sasquatch were always careful with was ensuring proper food production and consumption. The Sasquatch made sure they had proper food synthesizers matched to each dwelling, whether a doghouse or a house for a family of 12. The factory would consider all factors when it comes to matching the synthesizers. Since the synthesizers only used raw materials, like water, dirt, metals, and minerals, there was no need for refrigeration, just bins that are stored outdoors. Having adequate food and water is the most important thing for survival and emotional security, so that was where the biggest focus was for every dwelling. After that, they concentrated on the comforts.

The factory that made the synthesizers was the most closely monitored and featured the most human and Sasquatch workers. Although there were only 2 non-robots working at any time, which is more than any other Sasquatch factory, because almost every other factory doesn't have live workers. The usual day for the human and Sasquatch consists of three hours of walking around the factory, talking to the robot workers. The robot workers tell them if there are any issues in the building process, if they have any suggestions to make the process more efficient, or have thought of some way to make the product better. The factory work robots at the synthesizer plant were some of the smartest Sasquatch created, and continued to learn independently, after being programmed. The Sasquatch knew it was important to have robots that were capable of independent thought and capable of continued learning if they and the humans were going to be safe and continue to advance.

Dad's company began shipping the synthesizers to retailers. The only money the retailers were allowed to charge for the synthesizers was the amount it took to sell, deliver, and set them up. The Sasquatch wanted everyone to be able to afford a synthesizer. Once the first rush was over, and they could increase production, they would be able to give synthesizers for free to those that couldn't afford one, even at their inexpensive price. Once everyone had a synthesizer, they would save a massive amount of money thanks to not having to buy food, clothes, tools, or pretty much anything else... they could even synthesize a kitchen sink!

The Sasquatch synthesizers would make sure every human on Earth had food, water, clothes, and shelter. Also, because the synthesizers could make bricks and interlocking blocks, they could be used to build a shelter, if needed. Imagine having one in the desert! It could make water, food, and mirrored, insulated, interlocking blocks that could provide shade and shelter.

How about in the mountains? Or the North or South Poles? It would be easy for the synthesizers to create insulated blocks to build an igloo type structure anywhere on the planet.

The second most important factories were the ones that made power generating technology. The Sasquatch enjoyed having plenty of electrical power to drive their advanced technology. Virtually everything that required power was made with its own power generating capabilities built into its basic construction. Usually, the exterior material of the piece of technology was capable of generating sufficient power, but if that is not enough, then it could connect to a house or building to gain access to more. Most things in those homes generated their own power, but also drew from the house when needed. This included the computers, fans, blenders, TVs, and most other things.

9

SASQUATCH AND HUMAN KIDS
TOGETHER

Once the humans finished moving into the Sasquatch valley, they began setting up a learning center that utilized the advanced Sasquatch technology. The kids only needed to put on a special electronic helmet, which then transmitted the information directly to their brains. Once the information was uploaded to the kids' brains, they spent a few days talking about the subject matter in class in order to completely understand what they had been electronically taught. If they were taught a physical activity or skill—like judo, archery, ping pong, or skateboarding—then they needed to spend a few days establishing the needed muscle memory to perform those new skills.

Because of their extremely long lifespans, the Sasquatch understood the importance of social development, so they made sure all beings in their care enjoyed plenty of playtime with others. The Sasquatch designed learning centers to mimic various social environments, which encouraged individuals to want to learn more. All individuals enjoyed the advantages of their advanced technology and medical science.

The Sasquatch had the ability to extend lifespans almost indefinitely, and appreciated the importance of continued education and social involvement in maintaining optimal mental health. Before the Sasquatch would lengthen an individual's life expectancy, they made sure they had learned the proper life skills. There were therefore classes on exercise to maintain physical conditioning, so they could always be active even when they reached hundreds of years old. The Sasquatch had programs to learn to be a farmer, doctor, artist, musician, or even a spaceship pilot! Most beings that decided to live for centuries would change their life's direction many times. Noah used the learning centers many times, and took advantage of the anti-aging technology as well. His favorite was his drone training and being able to fly his dad into space.

The human and Sasquatch kids were taught in the same classrooms. It was decided to integrate the kids as early as possible, since they were going to be spending their lives together. The Sasquatch kids grew much larger, but they did so slower, so all the kids were of a similar size until the Sasquatch reached 18 or so and began to gain their full height and weight. A full-grown Sasquatch male can grow to 10 feet tall and 800 pounds, although most are only around 8 feet tall, and 600 pounds. An adult female will usually be between 7 and 8 feet tall and 500 to 700 pounds. Noah was encouraged to stop telling the other kids they could have their DNA changed so they could be as big and as hairy as a Sasquatch, because so many kept asking their parents if they could. A few of the parents suggested that they could increase the size of some kids and have a school football team. As much fun as that sounded, it was decided that—besides the fact that they would be cheating —it would draw too much attention to the valley and may threaten their privacy, since the Sasquatch were still not ready to reveal themselves to the world.

The classes the kids liked the most were the science and music classes. There was no limit to the knowledge available to be studied. The Sasquatch were millions of years ahead of humans in terms of technology. There were science classes in every discipline, including nuclear power, DNA, and sciences that humans had not even imagined yet. The humans that learned these super advanced sciences were instructed to never divulge any of the information to 'outside the valley' humans that had not been cleared to learn it.

All the students spent a few hours each morning in the learning centers. All the students then headed outside together to get some exercise, play, and eat lunch. Most of the kids then went on to do a bit of foraging, from which they would gather a couple of their favorite snacks for lunch. When it was outside playtime, many of the human kids would go into the rivers and ponds to swim. They all had their special Sasquatch-enhanced, self-inflating Carhartt coveralls, so they would be safe. Some of the braver Sasquatch kids wanted to swim like human kids, and pestered their parents enough that they designed self-inflating water wings that the Sasquatch kids could wear so they could play in the water with the kids safely. Looking out at the kids in the water, laughing and splashing, was always a fun social time shared between the Sasquatch and human adults.

As it turned out, some of the adult Sasquatch decided they wanted to swim also, so they produced a flotation vest that would fit an adult Sasquatch and keep their super heavy bodies afloat. The Sasquatch had always avoided water until they saw how much fun the humans had. Once their own Sasquatch kids started swimming and enjoying it, the adults wanted to try. Due to the weight of a Sasquatch, they would never be able to swim safely without a flotation aid of some sort. Despite this, many of the Sasquatch built shallow swimming pools for their homes because they enjoyed the water so much.

Noah wasn't against reminding people that, when he was fur covered and wet, he 'smelled like a wet dog', then he would stare at a Sasquatch in the water and laugh. It was at times like this that Mom realized no matter how much Sasquatch schooling he got, Noah was never going to grow up. That would mean he was very much like his grandpa and father, Mom thought, shaking her head.

When all the kids were on break in the woods, they tried to forage for food as much as possible. The Sasquatch had diligently planted the valley and surrounding land with plants that were edible and would produce year-round. It was heartwarming to watch the two different species gathering berries, mushrooms, and nuts together peacefully. It was also hysterical to watch them gather freshwater clams and crawfish. It does not matter how many hours training and working in a river you have, eventually you will slip and get washed downstream with flailing arms and legs, much to the delight of any onlookers!

After the kids gathered food, they prepared it and sat down together to eat. The Sasquatch only ate fruits, nuts, and vegetables, but they helped the humans gather the crawdads, clams, and fish. Eating together was an important part of Sasquatch culture, and the humans began thriving by sharing in their plentiful social life. Some of the adult humans that were working said that it was like they were retired, because they worked so few hours, and the work was so easy but also stimulating, and they got to spend so much time with their families and playing. Grandpa said he was in heaven being able to work in the Sasquatch labs, and that he would never retire completely.

Humans and Sasquatch kids are so similar in personality, that if it weren't for the Sasquatch body hair you couldn't tell them apart! Once the Sasquatch kids learned how to swim, the two groups spent most of their time together. The humans thought the Sasquatch kids were the most fun and interesting in the world, and the Sasquatch kids thought the human kids were the best ever. The two species of kids were like most young of their species, they wanted to play, and play they did. Whenever possible, the kids spent their time doing exactly that in the forest.

The Sasquatch kids only needed their water safety equipment and a safety communication device if they were going to stay in the forest. They didn't need any clothing, since they had such thick fur, so all they needed to do was build a nest to sleep comfortably. If a Sasquatch kid got hungry, they could forage for all their food and water. Noah's suggestion that the kids grow fur, so they didn't need their custom Carhartt's, made sense when camping with the Sasquatch. Sometimes, one of the bigger Sasquatch kids came alone, which made making sleeping nests easier. The bigger kids could bend bigger trees and branches together to make big nests where a dozen kids could sleep comfortably. The nights when the kids all slept in a huge nest were normally virtually sleepless nights, with lots of talking and laughing. Most of them then slept late into the afternoon, and awoke to parents making a big supper together nearby in a forest clearing.

10

SASQUATCH AND HUMAN LIVING TOGETHER

The Sasquatch would be the first to tell you that they have been living around humans for as long as their recorded history has existed. Their records indicate that there were times when humans were technologically equal with the Sasquatch, but then some natural cataclysm or war would happen, and humans would fall back into the Stone Age. The Sasquatch always waited until the trouble settled, then stepped back in to help humans climb back up. The Sasquatch knew that they and the humans shared a distant ancestor, so they felt we were brothers, and therefore have a shared responsibility to take care of each other.

One of the funnier things the Sasquatch have learned about humans, is how much they love cuddling with Sasquatch! They noticed the human need to cuddle furry animals, and some with no fur. It gives a good indication that humans are, at heart, a peaceful species. Once the humans lost their fear of the huge

Sasquatch, they wanted to cuddle, or even be carried, by them. That was Noah's favorite. Luckily, Sasquatch also love cuddling. There is nothing cuter than a 10-foot tall, 800-pound Sasquatch holding a tiny human baby in its massive hand! To be honest, even a full grown 200-pound man in the arms of a 10-foot tall 800-pound Sasquatch looks like a small child.

The Sasquatch, regard humans as still developing mentally. Much more intelligent than humans, as well as more patient, they are willing to teach the humans everything they needed to advance, both intellectually and technologically. Though they are regarded as much more than pets by the Sasquatch, since humans have the ability to match the Sasquatch intellectually, so the Sasquatch will spend the time to elevate the humans to their level. Human and Sasquatch history is long, and the Sasquatch say that our future together will be longer.

The Sasquatch are an extremely social species. They do not have names, because they feel everyone is equal, and that a name might lower or elevate someone's social status. All Sasquatch also work for the betterment of their species. That does not mean living the life any particular individual wants. It means that every Sasquatch makes sure they help rather than hurt. They share the workload, there is no such thing as money in their world. All Sasquatch feel that working together to build the community is the focus, rather than building wealth or power. That is why no Sasquatch company will charge money for their products. The Sasquatch feel pride in their accomplishment if they can provide for whoever is in need. The raw materials for the factories come from nature, so are free. The buildings, machinery, and factory infrastructure—including the robots—are grown, so they do not cost a thing, which means that all of the products the Sasquatch factories make cost nothing to make.

Many of the Sasquatch enjoy the tree homes, but like their fear of water, the Sasquatch have a fear of heights and can't climb trees. The massive size and density of the Sasquatch body means they will sink in water, so they have an inherent fear of it. The humans love of water has helped the Sasquatch to gain a new understanding and enjoyment of it. Similarly, the considerable size and weight of Sasquatch is the reason they do not normally climb trees... just imagine an 800-pound Sasquatch trying to stand on a tree branch! Now imagine 800 pounds falling because the branch broke. Since the Sasquatch grew tree homes for the humans, they decided to grow tree homes that were lower and stronger. A Sasquatch tree home looks like a short very fat Giant Redwood.

Sasquatch homes have only two rooms. First, they have a large main room, where they sleep, eat, entertain, and work. Then there is a side room that is the bathroom. For most of their existence, the Sasquatch have lived in caves. Living in a tree was never on their bucket list, but they have enjoyed the closeness with the forest that living in a tree provides. The Sasquatch believe that human kids playing with their kids has helped them experience the world more fully. The addition of tree living, swimming, and helping the humans hunt for food, granted Sasquatch kids a broader understanding. And the kids are having the best times of their lives together! The human kids talked the adults into adding zip-lines to connect the tree homes. At first, the Sasquatch were against it due to their size and understandable fear of falling, but it was pointed out that they could make super strong wires and harnesses that would hold even the biggest Sasquatch. It didn't take much convincing to get the Sasquatch kids to try the zip-lines. After seeing their kids use the zip-lines, all the adults wanted to try. The humans were lucky, because their Carhartt coveralls already had harnesses built in, and all they needed to do was clip their safety lines onto the cables and zip! The Sasquatch designed a harness that they could comfortably wear at all times, if they wanted, that also featured a built-in automatic flotation device so they could swim safely.

Throughout their recorded history, Sasquatch have never spent so much time playing as they do now that they are living with humans. They have always spent a great deal of time socializing, but this did not involve much playing. The Sasquatch claim it's the influence of the human kids, but Mom blames Grandpa for 'leading them all astray.' All you have to do is watch a 10-foot-tall 800-pound Sasquatch zip-lining at 30 MPH, laughing so loud you can hear them for miles, to realize that humans and Sasquatch mixing is a truly wonderful thing!

ABOUT THE AUTHOR

Patrick Talmadge Sr. has always been a late bloomer. His growth didn't cease until he was over 21 years old. He reached his pinnacle as a national and world-class masters middle-distance runner at the age of 37, when he won his first master's national track and field championship in the 800-meter run.

At 47, Patrick earned his Bachelor of Arts degree and made history as the oldest NCAA cross-country runner. Seven years later, at 54, he returned to college to pursue a Master's degree in Psychology. During this time, he ran the mile in track, once again setting a record as the oldest NCAA track and field runner. He received his Master's degree in Psychology at 57. At the age of 66, he embarked on his writing journey.

Patrick taught himself to read at the tender age of three and a half and has been an avid reader ever since. With a keen interest in all fields of science, science fiction, and fantasy, he amassed a wealth of knowledge that would later prove invaluable when he began writing. Throughout his 20s and 30s, Patrick devoured two to three books a day. Upon graduating from graduate school in 2011, he retired from competitive running and felt a growing desire to write the stories that had been simmering within him.

In November 2021, spurred on by the love of his life, Patrick began his writing career. By July 2023, he had completed an adult four-book science fiction series about Sasquatch, a four-book children's series on the same subject, and a standalone novel about a senior community that befriends a troupe of Sasquatch.

Patrick possesses a unique ability to write multiple stories simultaneously, allowing him to modify and adjust interconnected narratives for clarity when writing a series. With a bit of luck, Patrick will continue to pursue his passion for writing for the rest of his life, or at least until his computer gives out.

ALSO BY PATRICK TALMADGE

Hidden Mountain Chronicles

Sasquatch Race

Sasquatch Prison Diary

Tenino Caverns

Sasquatch Home Planet

Sasquatch Chronicles

Hunter and Noah vs. Sasquatch Vol. 1

Hunter and Noah vs. Sasquatch Vol. 2

Hunter and Noah vs. Sasquatch Vol. 3

Hunter and Noah vs. Sasquatch Vol. 4

Sasquatch Senior Community Series

Sasquatch Senior Community

Sasquatch Senior Community: Lois and Mel the Beginning

Sasquatch Senior Community: The Early Years

Sasquatch Senior Community: The Middle Years

AFTERWORD

Go to hangar1publishing.com to learn more about the Authors and stay up to date with their newest releases.

www.ingramcontent.com/pod-product-compliance
Lightning Source LLC
Chambersburg PA
CBHW061324120626
46546CB00007B/2669